TIN CAN TROUBLE

PSS!

PRICE
STERN
SLOAN

PRICE STERN SLOAN LIMITED, NORTHAMPTON, ENGLAND

It was early morning in the land of
Do-As-You're-Told.

Over on the dump, Stoppit was about to go out to play – when an old tin can shuffled by. All on its own!

Stoppit decided to have some fun.
He jumped up onto the tin.

The tin moved on, over the bridge and up the hill, towards Tidyup's.

Tidyup had been busy that morning making himself a garden table.

He wanted to sit outside in the sun
to eat his gherkin sandwiches.

It was then that Stoppit bounced into the garden on the old tin can.

Tidyup was surprised! A tin can that moved! And made funny noises!

He had to find out what was inside.
He picked up the tin and shook it.

And out fell an odd-looking shell.
What could it be? It started to twitch
– and a leg popped out.

Of course! It was Don't-Do-That!

Oh dear! Tidyup knew that meant trouble. Don't-Do-That was a pest!

First he climbed on to Tidyup's roof.
Tidyup tried to get him down, but,
just as he reached him . . .

Don't-Do-That jumped off and ran
into the gherkins.

Next he hid in the tallest gherkin in the garden and started throwing little tree gherkins down at them.

Stoppit thought it was funny . . .

. . . until one hit him on the head.

Tidyup decided that was enough.

He must do something. But what?
Then a tree gherkin hit him too.

And that gave him a bright idea.

Stoppit quietly sawed away at the big gherkin . . .

. . . while Tidyup kept Don't-Do-That busy throwing tree gherkins.

The plan worked . . .

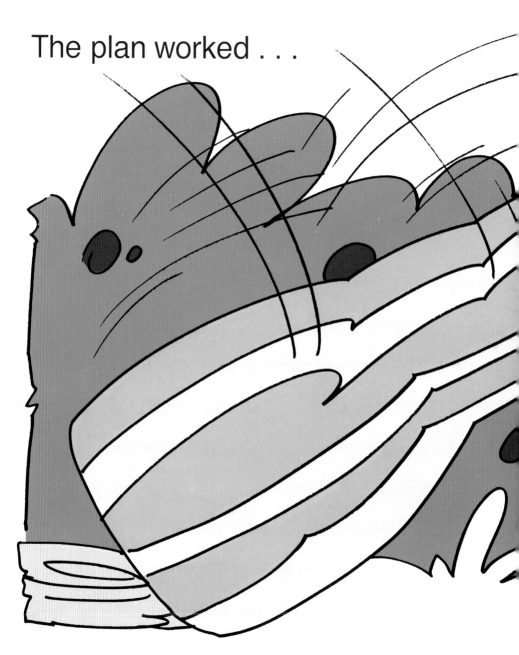

The gherkin fell. Don't-Do-That was so surprised he popped back into his shell. But Tidyup's new table was smashed to pieces.

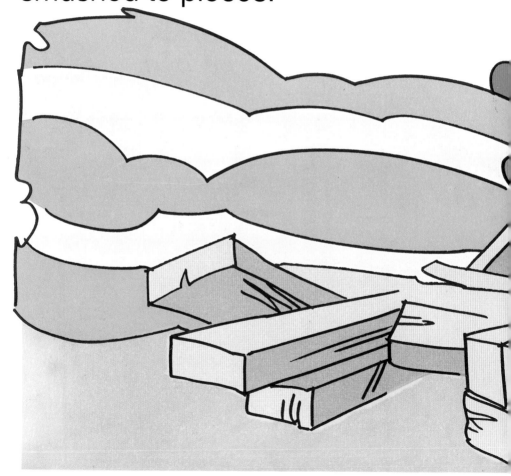

Stoppit jumped on top of the shell.
Don't-Do-That had had enough.

He scuttled off, taking Stoppit with
him. That made Tidyup smile.

And Tidyup did manage to eat outside in the sun after all. He used the sawn-off gherkin as a garden table.